The Heart and the Subsidiary

Fatima Al Matar

authorHOUSE®

AuthorHouse™ UK Ltd.
500 Avebury Boulevard
Central Milton Keynes, MK9 2BE
www.authorhouse.co.uk
Phone: 08001974150

First published by AuthorHouse 2/2/2010

ISBN: 978-1-4490-6936-0 (sc)

Acknowledgment

I am grateful to my dear friend and poet Mr. Fred Holland
for reading and revising my poetry.
Always just an e-mail away whenever I needed guidance,
support and sound judgment.

For My Beautiful Daughter

Jori

Contents

Preface

Anne Radcliff: Of what do you wish to write?

Jane Austen: Of the heart.

Anne Radcliff: Do you know it?

Jane Austen: Not all of it.

An exchange from when Jane Austen was still a young aspiring writer at a meeting with her heroine Anne Radcliff.

Mother
Daughter

'The best mothers are those who remember what it was like when
they themselves were young daughters'

The author

Until you have a child

You see the healthier,
                    cleaner,
                             purer,
part of your soul
in higher definition,
gleaming
in a shape of a smaller
human,
dancing in a pink ballet tutu,
running towards the school gate.

And all you want is
to reserve it,
maintain It,
watch in wonder
how there is
a better version
of yourself.

The different sides of love
constantly revolving,
you are amazed
at love's
endless hues,
and the constant eternal
state of worry it brings.

When they are ill
with the cruellest,
or the slightest
illness,
you are ready to be the comfier
bed,
stroking your cool hand against
their warm forehead

'God, please spare her'
echoes through
the sleepless nights
until
you have reach the very basement of
your aching heart
you are between the
inner walls of love
where its beats
maroon
delicate, slippery
and lonely.

Don't say 'I love you'
until you have a child

REDUNDANT

I told her what a horrible mother she was
I numbered all her bad judgements
her shortfalls
her inefficiencies,

I reminded her of all that she was lacking
how miserable she made me through the years
how ignorant she has been
I furiously told her
that I hated her.

I thought about this,
when they placed you into my arms
the very first time
surrounded by smiling faces
I whispered in your ear
'I'm the only one who knew you before you were
born'.

I had thought about this
when I carefully rested your tiny head
close to my heart,
you feet dangled no lower than my waist
I wondered impatiently
what your voice would sound like.

I had thought about it
when you had your first vaccination,
I felt the cruel prick
as the cold needle invaded your baby skin,
the untouched virgin flesh interrupted
by manmade drug

now,
you let go of my hand in haste,
crossing the road recklessly
eager to join your friends
on the other side
careless to even glimpse my way
I gasp in amazement,

I had planned to compensate you by now,
for all my poor judgments,
all my inefficiencies
my ignorance

     the lacking,

but the years had passed
as I stand here

redundant.

I NEVER THANKED YOU

I never thanked you for being born

whole,

Ten perfect little fingers
Ten perfect little toes.

I never thank you for being a healthy baby
coming out through the right passage way
as opposed to
having them cut through my insides,
and force you out

I never thanked you for not shoving a penny up your
nose,
making me drive you to the hospital at 1 am

or making that embarrassing apologetic phone call
after you had bit another child in school

I never thank you for any of these things,

Instead I took all credit for how lovely and well
behaved you are,
I complained about how demanding you can be
sometimes,
I complained about your terrible 2 to 3 tantrums,
I said you were a handful, and how I
miss my pre-mothering days

But in my loneliest, coldest nights
I quietly creep into your bedroom and lie beside you
I listen to you breath,
you beautiful, perfect face
pressed against the warm pillow.

such fulfilling peace.

You were new

When you were born, you were new
fingers folded inwards,
in a tiny fist,
your nails, as tender as skin,
your eye lids sleepy, too heavy to lift up
your crying was tearless, as if tears only came with
reason
and you had none
your weeping was the mere call for attention
even when there were tears
they were little drops of morning dew
pure from any grief,
untainted with life's regrets.

You only grinned and chuckled peacefully in your
sleep,
a time for the rest of us full of concern.

Everything pink, the colour of uncooked meat,
the blend of more whites than reds
before the red slowly, malignantly encroaches.

Everything soft,
smoothly curved,
no sharp edges
no rigidness.

Born with the heavenly smell of new blessings
a life time of so much possibility,
surrounded by smiling, pastel coloured,
stuffed animals.

Protected from the wind,
the noise,
even the sunlight was too strong
on your raw eyes.
Soon there will be fences
up and down the stairs
soon there will be a special car seat
and anti-germ sprayed everywhere.

My elbow tests your warm,
pre-sterilized bath water,
your sponge without the dry fibrous side
your skin too rare to exfoliate.

How long will I be able to shelter you?
how long can I maintain you green?
before I'm compelled to let you step outside
exposed to harshness.

Her Anger

I remember her anger,
her frustration with a husband that was never there.
I close my ears shut when I recall her crying,
or murmuring things I was too little to understand.

I remember the sadness,

how familiar it was
and how
we have grown old together,
how it still comes to lie beside me
stroking my hair lovingly:
'It's alright I'm here'

Now I treat it like a survey sample
listing my unhappiness on pages,
crossing the ones I had already questioned
or the ones I naively thought I had overcome

and pretended

I have pretended for years
waiting for my heart to play along

took all suggestions on board,

   prayed,
    moved house,
     said pretentious things like:
      'motherhood is wonderful'

but it never came

security.

Three

She was three,
and the star of her very first nursery play
'The Star Who Couldn't Twinkle'

She came out in a golden star costume amongst other
starry children,
petrified by the number of unfamiliar faces gawking,
waiting for her to utter her first line,

her big brown eyes,
rounded,
widened,
and swiftly ran past all the faces that were not mine.

Her fragile, racing heart trembling like a lost kitten's
trying to find its way home in the dark.

Then her eyes suddenly fell on mine,

they clenched,

she gazed at me, still frightened and without a word
she seemed to say:
'Will you make it less frightening?'

Three years ago,
the very first moment they placed her into my arms,
screaming, terrified, and dripping of blood
she didn't know who she was,
she didn't know who I was,
but she confided in me,
her eyes rounded,
widened,
she looked straight into my eyes,
our eyes clenched,
and without a word,
she seemed to ask:

'Will you make it less frightening?'

and I,

in my new, hasty, motherly love
ignorantly nodded
yes.. yes.. yes..

LANGUAGE

Throughout our years of war,
the arguments
the different languages we spoke
you turned away so many times,
I hated you for not understanding

Now I sit, with my legs bent
She stands with her back facing me
I clutch her tiny waist between my thighs
and run the brush through her thick dark hair
repeating your hand motion.
I don't sing,
she doesn't speak,
we let the brush between us straighten all.

This must be how you felt
every time you clutched me
between your thighs
you'd tell me to stand still
I'd tilt my head backwards
the brush would run from
the top of my skull
all the way down.
a strange sensation ran through
my bones,
my heavy eye lids drop.

As I grew taller
I had to kneel on my knees
I grew taller still, until
you had to stand.

This must be how you felt

That no matter how much
you loved me,
I was never entirely yours,
and no matter how tall I grew
there would always be
untamed thick dark hair
that needed restraint.

WINTER MORNING

It was a cold winter morning,

I taught her how to hold the edges of her cuffs with
her tiny fingers
while I screwed another woolly jumper into her head,
pulling her arms through a second pair of sleeves,
the rim of the undergarment slightly peeking through

I wanted to spare her the discomfort of the first sleeve
pulled up,
and gathered at her elbow.

She was almost three, and delighted with the new
discovery
she did it every morning since:

'Shall I let go now mummy?'

Love makes us do that,
spare them the discomfort of things,
life's little troubles,
the small anxieties often over looked.

I wondered how many of life's discomforts I'll be able
to spare her,
and whether my remedies will continue to delight
her,
I wondered whether I would have the remedy at all.

The Beautiful Woman

Her thick long mahogany hair
with its large luscious curls
sat on her chest beautifully
very gently,
rising and falling,
rising and falling
as she breathed.
They bounced to the most
alluring rhythm when she
walked.
accenting her speared eyes
her perfectly sculptured lips
and the coat of milky smooth
skin,
emphasised her voluptuous
curves.

Whenever he was gone
on a mysteriously long
business trip,
She'd look down on me
her captivating eyes
raging:

'It's your father you take after,
with your big nose, and your
masculine hands'.

I cried,
growing up ashamed of my
ugly nose and manly hands,

I watched her
as she sat before the mirror
in misery
analysing her
beauty
burdening her long delicate
neck with chains of
shimmering gold,
unhappy

as if she was contained
in her faultless exterior

now her beauty fades
in prejudice speed
and she laughs
setting her wrinkles free.
Her life is full
now that the curves are lost
and the luscious hair is thin;
released from her enslaving
endowments.

She sits surrounded by
adoring grandchildren
leaning on her retired
contented husband
of 32 years.

It's easy to love you now

I scrub the crayons off the walls
then move on to clean water colours off the new
carpet
on my knees,
I lift my head up in between dabs of water and soup
that have now turned purple from all the
reds and blues you have splashed everywhere
I catch a glimpse of green peas shoved under the sofa.
the empty bag of sweets which I earlier said you
should not have,
is placed carefully in the bin
covered with clean sheets of tissues.

After a long day of hoovering,
yelling,
and laborious bathing
determined to get the orange paint out of your nose
I think of how tired you make me,
and how life was quiet and simple before you came
how I sat elegantly painting my flowers,
how cleaning was something I did occasionally,
how I slept through the night,
lunched with friends,
and had long, uninterrupted phone conversations.

How you exhausted those pleasures in me
and brutally demanded all my time, thought and
attention
how at the end of even your best behaved days
I lie shattered.

You're finally in bed now
you close your eyes
clean and smelling of apple blossom shampoo
your rosy cheeks warm against the pillow
your full lips pressed and pouting
so peaceful
your brown soft hair, still damp
I sit beside you
stroke my fingers against your face
whispering a prayer
you smile in your sleep

Why is it so easy to love you now?
everything,
all the effort
is worthwhile now.

LONG DISTANCE

It's true,
the more similar you are
the harder
communication becomes.

The lifelong discontentment
with one's self,
staring back,
pronounced,
bitter from
disownment.

Although I will never be
as brilliant as you,
your sharp intellect,
you undeniable wit,
your vast achievements.

I can think of a million things to say
none are suitable,
and there's always an
annoying echo
of my voice
through the
cracking
long distance phone call

When I think of
us
of all the conversations
we could have had,
filling all the wasted silences,
petty moments of anger
when we disagreed.

Everyday
I know
another day is lost
and that I'm
running out of time.

You call,
the line breaks,
and the silences unfilled.

It always ends the same

'I'm fine,
the weather is lovely,
thanks for calling
Dad'.

SHOULDERS

'Hold on to mummy's shoulders'

As mummy stretched the elastic
  waist of a pair of Winni the Pooh pyjama trousers.

She,
concentrated hard,
keeping balance on one foot,
while trying her best to
aim at sinking the other
into the first hole,
missing the first couple of times.

Mummy stiffens her shoulders further,
as the tiny chubby hands squeeze harder.

'Come on Mr. Foot!'
She giggles playfully,
in her four year old angelic voice.

Mummy's eyes drowning;
    soon she'll be able to pull them up
    effortlessly.

The author (1 year old) carried by her mother in Stirling (Scotland) 1981

The author carrying her daughter Jori (2 years old) in Coventry UK 2007

Inspired

'Inspiration is a very busy woman'

the author

You let us

Love,
You come without definition,
without shape,
without colour.

You could be anything
the smell of incessant, mysterious oceans
to those lives restricted
by a fence.

You could be what lies between
a crescent moon
and its Venus,
in an intimate convergence
to those
who confuse stars with planets.

How many times did we use you?
Abuse you?
We ignorantly place you,
we insert you
where you don't belong
to justify our lowly human ways.

and you let us

Every religion turns your face to a different god,
but you are never 'god'
Every gender ties you to its own erotic desires,
to call lust by your name

and you let us

We blame the fragile heart shaped
pump inside us,
we claim that that is where we stuff you
and that is where you hurt us the most

and you let us

and when the fragile heart shaped pump fails us
we don't mention you at all

and you let us

We say
you are the bud of all happiness,
then we say
you are the root of all misery,
with no more than mere minutes gapping
our absurdity.

and you let us

We pray you will find us,
than we complain how you are blind

and you let us

Maybe you are just
a person without a god, without a gender
living alone in the woods
walking your dog every afternoon
laughing,
at my silly poetry.

For Poetry

Trollop

Why is it you only come in the night?
As if carrying a shameful secret,
as if you'd rather no one knew about us.

You come to dance on my plain white
vain letterheads,
revealing no more than your bare feet
like a trollop,
each poem you write is a new charming man
who contains you,
and leaves you wondering how you've ever
considered settling for his predecessor.

Your insatiability is my muse,
but it is often not what you make me write
but what you restrain;
a few inkblots,
tolerating myriad analysis
opening the flood gates to interpretation.

But I will never preclude
your inconvenient, suspicious visits in the dark
your homonym wink from under your
un-pierced veil.

APPLE

She was two,
still trying to master the art of walking
she pulled my dress, and said:

"Mummy apple"

I handed her a small red apple
She took it, then quickly gave it back to me

"Mummy open it"

Maybe it`s human nature to open things
doors, presents, hearts.

The excitement of the surprise,
the adrenaline rush of not knowing what to expect,
the optimistic lift when believing we would find what
we hoped for

Until,
    doors close,
        presents disappoint,
            hearts mislead.

"It turns men on, they pay incredible amounts of money for it, and it's one of the largest industries in the country. If women got as much out of pornography as men do, we would buy it instead of cosmetics, which is a massive industry in its own right, for which women are a market, we spent our money to set our selves up against the objects that emulate those images that are sold as erotic to men. The only message that pornography sends is that we enjoy degradation that women are sexually turned on by being degraded".

Catharine A. Mackinnon (feminist)
From her book 'Feminism Unmodified'

HOOR VS. WHORE

I wanted to love my religion,
in fact I tried very hard to love my God
the very same way I tried very hard to love my
husband
but one way or the other they have betrayed me
every minute of every passing day I was judged on:
how small my waist
how full my lips
how round my breast?
these were not questions addressed to me,
they were mere requirements
I simply had to fulfil.
The threshold was already set, high, and long before I
was conceived
Allah created Hoor,
72 of which were rewarded to each pious worshiping
Muslim man
Allah's male scholars defined their heavenly Hoor as:

'chaste females, with wide beautiful eyes, untouched,
unbroken by sexual intercourse, like pearls, virgins,
voluptuous/full-breasted, non-menstruating/non-
urinating, non-defecating and childfree, round breasts
which are not inclined to hang, transparent to the
marrow of their bones, eternally young, hairless, pure,
beautiful, white, re-virginating, splendid'.

In short Hoor is everything a real earthly woman isn't.
The God whom I have worshiped blindly
condemned me to a life time of constant tolerance to
one man's deficiencies
yet he does not promise me an impeccable male in a
heaven that I must eagerly await.
Neither did man let me live serving him,
pleasing him with a vision of an eternally young,
eternally virgin female clouding my sky
in a heaven which he had created till death do us part,

No,

Instead he sentenced me to live competing against my
own reflection,
of which I had no choice,
took my insecurities and pinned them against the
wall,
in glossy posters and tasteless pictures in cheap
magazines,

my lust a virtue,
my flesh available,
I live confused,
resembling neither the sinless hoor
nor the promiscuous whore.

I say now
if I must try to love you
then it is simply
not love.

Hoor, or Hoor Alayn, is a term the Qu'ran gives to heavenly women rewarded to pious Muslim men in paradise, the Qur'an mentions 'Hoor' repeatedly e.g. Surat Al Waqiah, verse 56:22 – 23.

More

This sadness with its worn out bent edges
I lie in the middle of it and stretch my arms and legs
making snow angels
trying to expand it
wanting more room
tired of this stiffness in the heart
longing for more:
more time
more life
more happiness
and more of the light, flexible, ease in which I used to
tread
when uncertainly was exciting.

SHADOW AND LIGHT

She sits patiently,
painting flowers in vases
striving to master shadow and light
determined to make a non-existent seem real.

She then carries her flat replicas
displays them for everyone to see
smiles pretentiously and says:
'Yes, I'm quite proud of this one'

As her sorrows watch from a distance
nodding proudly at every masterpiece
holding her hand back home
                when it's all over
wrapping her warm in bed,
telling her favourite bed time story,

'Once you have perfected
            shadow and light
                all will be real'.

Death

I always pictured it somewhat like leaving nursery
school,
being pulled away from the sounds I was most
familiar with,
kind faces I had grown used to.

Exiting the cosy, colourful class room,
the small corners where I sulked,
when my mother and I parted
that first day
one of us willingly
the other averse.
How her deliberate abandonment
astonished and wounded me,

how the teacher let me cry it off
alone,
by myself

she continued so casually
with the other children
who had already made the transition,
                                    crossed the barrier,
                                    exited the doors,
they carried on so cheerfully.

Taken away from everything I had known,
the pillows I stack against my back
to comfort me,
while I read in bed.
The yellow tea roses
I place on my dressing table
to cheer me up
in the morning.

Being air lifted from my every belief,
every little concept of life

'She'll come around'
  my teacher assured my mother
'some of them adapt sooner than others'

Paradox

In the unsettling, startling darkness
there is serenity
there is calmness
there is a peace

as there is discomfort in day
as there is impairment in light

as some satisfactions can be agitating
as some agitation can be satisfying

through my glass window I see beyond my self
in the daylight
the window exposes life
there is grass, sun and sky
I see people holding each other,
I see them letting go.

In the late hour the
lucid glass
closes life
and reflects
self.

For my dearest and darling friend
Anna Varghese Puthuran.

SHE WRITES POETRY

She writes poetry.
She doesn't have the patience for novels
any more,
It takes a lot of heart
to create two people and make them fall in love
It takes a juvenile imagination to create for them
the perfect happiness
and she had neither

Impatience spreads.

She doesn't give men the chance to look
and admire her from a far,
her one track mind
can only measure broad shoulders,
long lean backs,
stiff masculine abs,
and tight hinds.

When she invites a man over
she tells him to bring a tooth brush.

She feels a strong satisfaction in riding the train
taking her efficiently from where she is to where
she wants to be
fast.
No traffic lights,
no wheel to steer,
no fateful cross roads to chose from,
or clever shortcuts to learn by heart,
she doesn't have to concentrate,
or fill up the gas.
She doesn't make an effort
at all.

On a beautiful morning
when the moon refuses to fall
abandons night and stars,
longs for the sun's warmth,
she realizes that all rules can be broken.

She sits now to write a love poem
but it doesn't come
all the men she loved

quickly
efficiently
were strangers.

After John Berryman
'Address to the Lord'

HANDS

God,
All I need is to raise these hands before my eyes
to stand in wonderment and amazement
these hands
these magnificent hands
that can hold,
fold,
stretch,
and grasp.

Cool on my child's feverish forehead
warm on a lover's face
gentle on your weaker creatures
firm as I hold my pen.

Such insight
Such genius

Not one finger, dispensable
Neither works without the other.

In such harmony and immediate
understanding, one stirs
while the other carefully follows
a cook book recipe

Both knitting
crossing paths in complexity
not one disturbing the other
in quietness and peace.

Translating our thoughts
Miming our hindered emotions
Portraying nature's brilliance
in unique individuality.

Two incredible diligent executors of
our body's intentions

These hands
these magnificent hands
some have trained animals
some transplanted human hearts
some have written books
and some speak a language
when voices are lost.

And still they surprise me,
and still I stand in astonishment
humbled
by their unbounded skills.

God,
O, divine creator
How can I not love you?
How can I not kneel before you?
My master
Craftsman of beauty.

'I didn't want be like Yeats,
I wanted to be Yeats'.
John Berryman

For my aunt Aisha
who died of cancer in 2004.

BENIGN

When the cancer took.
You gracefully unknotted
the tangled emotions.
You slowly and gently unwrapped
love.
You untied its tether,
as if you have saved some spring
for the long indefinite winters.

You gazed at your
daughters condoling faces,
recorded
every expression
while
the sick swamp green
cells multiplied,
you wondered in silence
how can death breed
in such frightening speed?

You were astounded
at how lack of time
suddenly
breathed enchantment
into everything
you took for granted,
at how only lack of time
can make a moment
last.

You promised your youngest
that you'd meet again
in a heaven
where only the benign
multiply.

Funny this life.
Only when we are
asked to hand back the
keys, do we realize,
we never even took the time
                    to unlock the doors.

ABOUT THE SADNESS

I wanted to tell you about the sadness
that came knocking every night
pounding on my heart
begging,
longing to be let back in,
it often sat beside me,
handing me my pen,
the desperate cry to be acknowledged

write,
write,
it whispered,

take it,
take the loneliness,
the tears
the empty fullness you live by everyday
and love me
and write me on the pages
so I can live, and breed,

writing it
meant giving it a face,
describing it
meant allowing it lips to speak
there's no telling what it might say
no telling if it will ever stop.

I have created this monster
that snarls,
and roars,
I have given it its name
the anger that runs it wild
the cuts and bruises it feeds on,
the painful love that won't be put to sleep
the lifelong doubts that keep it certain,
the lacking that keeps it coming for more.

for Suad.

HAPPINESS

Happiness,
when they took you
they raped,
deformed,
then stabbed you
34 times.
They split your limbs,
electrocuted your flesh;
until it was blue in some places
and black in others.
ditched your disconnected body
at the front gate of your house
for your mother to find
in the morning.
stinking and
covered with flies,
punched with holes from when they
used you as an ashtray.

They didn't hurt you.
When they thought they took your life
they thought wrong.

They urinated inside you,
then they stepped on your stomach
and laughed at the sound of their waste
spurting out.

But when they really wanted to have fun,
they squeezed tiny, diseased ,hungry, mice
into your vulva,
scratching their way through
your vagina
they fed on your uterus.

Your surviving inmates explained.

Told us the stories after the war
about the dungeon black
torture.
For seven months
they begged to be killed
longing for your fate.

survivors?

All of them still strapped
to their psychiatric chairs
suicidal,
ruined by every form and level of
degradation.
they twist in agony
when governments
kiss, hold hands
'The war is behind us'.
they murmur cowardly.

Happiness,
you'll never have to relive the
pain.
None of us survived the war
the way you did.

Suad was a 20 year old law student at Kuwait University when Iraq invaded
Kuwait in 1990. She was captured by Iraqi soldiers tortured to the most
inhumane level then dumped in front of her home in the night, her mother
finding her an unrecognisable corpse in the morning. Her name 'Suad' is the
equivalent of the word 'Happiness' in English.

Abused

'When we minimize abuse, it becomes our way of living'

The author

Black Widow

Every time the playground gate swings open,
Every time the playground gate swings shut,
The eight legged widow spins her silken web.

The estranged wife sits on a wooden bench
on a cold windy day
watches her daughter play

carefree.

A yellow, ramshackle, dying leaf hanging
desperately to a thin dry twig
on a mighty tree
catches her eyes.

The wind blew
stronger
the wind blew
colder,
but the dying leaf lingered.
The wife thought silently
'maybe it's time to let go'

She recalls
how after his constant abuse
she was time and time again
thrown out her own home
in the cold night
bare footed,
wearing very little.

it is time to let go
it is time to let go

Because anything is better than this
because anything is better than waiting to be
dropped from life
discarded,
dumped,

and yet every time the playground gate swung open,
every time the playground gate swung shut
The repeatedly made homeless widow
spun her silken web.

CONTRACEPTION

The doctor cuts through her arm
as he chats casually to the nurse,
fits a plastic implant under her skin,
the sound of two layers of flesh parting
damp, and hesitant
like the sound of detaching a snail
stuck firmly to a surface.

Her mind drifts,
images of her husband's cruelty,
sounds of her mother screaming
'I wish I never had any of you'
and the fragility of what are now
her barren eggs
helplessly wasting.

She leaves the clinic
head down,
shaking,
and drowsy
drives herself home,
with an effort.

The anaesthetic starts to wear off
she can now feel how deep the knife
sunk.

STAINS

The day you left,
I gave all your Gucci shoes to charity.

It was cleaning the oven day,
your Armani shirts finally came in handy.

And then there was the lime scale on the toilet seat

well,

your Dunhill suits worked wonders there.

I tied all your Hugo Boss ties together,
and used them as a line for my washing.

But there was that nasty stain on the carpet
from the time when you
Slapped
the coffee mug from my hand
in rage and anger

some stains are

permanent.

BUTTERFLY

You didn't leave room for regret;
the all shades of grey
never white,
never black,
revolting,
post traumatic feeling
that finds comfort only between the eyes
and their lids,
in the night when desperate for sleep.

There were no pieces to pick up
no contact details to delete
nothing was lost.
Even the chaffy scales left over
by your harsh threshing of the skin
were refined,
and blown way
by a calm, cruel breeze
called abandonment

The caterpillar that fed on a green luscious leaf
cocooned.

After me,
you are still an ugly insect
only this time you were enhanced.
You flew away with a pair of colourful majestic wings.

DUSTING SKIN

Four years ago
she did not imagine this ending
dusting the bed sheets from
dead skin his body shed last

is this how all loveless marriages end?

In quietness
as dark and pale as the night they wed.

Through the years
searching for a valid emotion
that can hold this
ton weighed ogre.

For a coat peg
sturdy enough to bear
      tearless goodbyes,
          robotic embraces,
              feeling of shameful invasion
following scarce foreign love making.

Love,

How did I stagger this farther away from you?
how long did you imagine I could es, es, stammer my
lines eluding you?
how did I reduce immense aspirations into a trivial
diamond ring?
what was my estimate of my heart's shelf life?

Not four.

ORIGAMI

In her attempt to master the art of origami
she has taken this thin, brittle love,
and folded it into
an eagle
she dreamt it would one day soar.

but after so many years
of being pressed
under his inflated ego
his vulgar need for dominance.
his deluding skills,
reducing her to more insecurities,
to more doubt.
his intimidating, coercive threats
feeding on her vulnerability,
sucking on her
fragility.

She doesn't cry,
some cruelties are beyond tears,
some unhappiness beyond threshold.

She has come to understand
now, that a paper bird
can never fly,
and the dead skin
that forms under a neglected foot
in ill shades of yellow
even when eagerly hanging
to the living,
will never truly be alive.

She will not let him empty his dark,
barbaric desires inside her any more.
She will not wither and shrivel to fatten his
sick need for self worth.
She will not continue to be mislead by
his wicked virtual denial.

and this smothered heart,
this long-deprived,
smothered heart,

will rise.

HEARTS IN RECESSION

Words, re-used over and over
until empty and finished,
praises, scarce.
flirtation, expensive and postponed indefinitely.

Sleeping apart is more comfortable by the day,
we live together,
but I hardly ever notice you are there.

'You're wasting too much electricity'
I shout,
you answer me with slammed doors.

Ironing your shirts is a job,
for which I feel I'm extremely underpaid.

I think of you,
of our life together
how little you have rewarded my giving,
you like to remind me of your kind gestures
and claim to deduct them off your bill.

They are small, and far apart,
they are mere expenses of the profits
you've made,
your balances are inefficient and your taxes are
overdue,
your constant emphasis of ancient sacrifices
is shameful and demeaning.
I say.

When we argue,
I scream 'why can't you just be someone else'
then I cry because you have no idea what I mean

but I do.

PILL

I take you like a pill
Reluctant,
compelled.

I press you through the
thin, silver, metallic sheet

there's a comic yet evil
sound to you piercing through
the malleable metal foil,
always taking some of the
health warning in bold print,
as you go

20 mg capsules of chemical
substance I am unable to
pronounce,
your ridiculously long
complex name is an emphasis
of your hazardous
effects

You pop out so easily
but that is not how you
go down;
you need to be pushed
thrust, forced down my
throat.

I feel you tumbling heavily
bumping, blindly into
the interior walls of the canal
the hollow tube
my muscular chamber
where my vital air
and food passages
cross

I realize
there's no turning back now;
I have let you in,
and must bear the consequences

I feel you twisting, turning
upside down,
sideways
I can never be sure
on which face you have landed.

Shadows

She dreads the sight of his shadow expanding
on the glass front door.
He's back from work.
Her heart sinks into a pool of deep depression
rotten with unhappiness,
moldy with fear

When he grabs her after he
has shoved her around,
the illusive shadow on the walls
reflects a loving couple
embracing.

When he forces her into his bed
The vague shadows on the ceiling
show no signs of struggle.
show no tears.

He slaps her to the floor,
she gently strokes the carpet
in a powerless,
repeated hand motion
trying to find her glasses,
the baby robin fallen out of its
nest with its swollen purple blue eyes

helpless.

She wraps her arms around her wasted
skinny self.
The shadow on the floor
still deceiving,
is the shape of a stubborn,
mountain rock.

She wishes she can
shed this bruised skin.
She wishes she can
peel off this battered flesh.
To rewire her troubled mind
She wishes she could detach her body
from this
molested soul.

Box

He found a cardboard box
the heavy load it had been bearing for so
many years
has left its edges torn and slightly folded
outwards.
Soggy, and worn out
due to the many times
it had been left out in the rain.

'That'll do for now'
He said.

In it,
he emptied all his
waste,
burdened it
with everything
worthless to him
the shabby
the flimsy
all that was
not elegant enough
to hang on the walls
or display on the shelves.

Then,
when he no longer needed the box
he took a blade
and swiftly slit
down the corners,
with zero resistance
the exhausted sides
tumbled,
surrendering to their lifelong
abuse.

'That way, it won't take too much room in the trash'
He thought proudly to himself.

The skill of disposing.

After Love

We are never the same after love.
The fragile moth captured by its delicate wings, twitching.
Our rubbed off velvety scales
forever lost.
Our detainers finger tips
forever stained.

We spent what's left of our years fluttering
around the glowing bulb
drawn to artificial warmth.

The author

PEBBLE

I'm merely a pebble on your shore
your waves indifferently turn me
face up
face down
sideways,
whatever suits you best on that particular day,
moment
you make of me what pleases you
you interpret me to your own selfish liking
you forget me
your waves toss me dry on a lonely sandbank,
thirsty
years passing by
you remember me once more
your waves slowly crawling closer
not wanting to seem obvious, that you miss me
licking the salty sand to where your waves last left me
you are certain I'd still be there
I foolishly accept their doubtful, reluctant tail.

I remember how once I had a few sharp edges,
an uneven surface
how once I was
difficult
but drowning in you has smoothened all

all is clear
all is easy.

IN-DISPOSABLE

I don't know what to do with these feeling any more,
I've tried painting them, and repainting them.
then I did what any woman would do,
heavy textured, loud print vinyl,
but the poor plastering job did not hold.

I re-cycled them into something, even I failed to
recognize,
and gave them to another man,
but they were sent back to me,
damaged,
more complex.

I shoved them around like an overweight suite-case
in a busy air-port,
I left them well unattended, within easy access,
hoping to get mugged,
excess baggage, has proven an unappealing
commodity.

I finally crumpled, and crinkled them into a creased,
uneven shape and tossed them
carelessly in the bin sitting next to my desk,
the way a writer chucks away
a disappointing page.

I heard them slowly unfold,
the disturbing, haunting sound of wrinkled, dry
paper
creeping back from the dead

my in-disposable sadness.

Lessons

She demonstrates to her heart
how water gladly takes the shape of a jug
then almost instantly adapts to the shape of a
drinking glass.

She shows it how sugar willingly dissolves
stirred gently or roughly,
quickly or slowly.
into the warm cup of tea

Look,

look how red calmly surrenders to violet
when brushed against blue,
without any resistance turns to orange when
encountered
by hostile yellow,
changes mood, character
submits to sensuous maroon when dominated by
authoritative black,
and yet devoted to innocent baby pink when
resigning to sinless
white.

How a tulip bulb will grow exactly where it was
planted,
and when moved with care to another garden,
continues to grow and flourish.

How fresh cream can be spread on bread,
                    spooned and served with cake, or
                        poured on top strawberries,

She explains, trying to convince her reluctant heart
how resilience can be a virtue
not to be tethered by painful love,
to be shaped and reshaped,
the flexibility to be contained,
    stretched, or
        fenced might be good for both of us, she added

she feels it seethe with anger when someone recklessly
says:

'anything can be fixed'
'anything can be done'

You are my autumn

You are my autumn.
You come back to me always.

Hushing down the summers,
paving the way for the dreary rain

Unlike the other seasons,
you are silent,
the fusion of inevitability and doubt.
I walk in the woods looking up
waiting for the first sign of an orange leaf
anticipating the beautiful death of trees.

The grasses whisper amongst themselves
in the colder than usual breeze

You come so casually,
we speak as if we have never parted
and just as I have started yielding
the long awaited crimson leaves
I am standing against a strong current
of harsh cold winter winds

holding your memory near

Half Moon

Half moon
hid behind half lit black clouds,
in an evening
still,

not quite late,
not appropriate to call

or do I always find an excuse?
I say: 'life will find a way'
but this is the same mature moon
at which you and I gaze,
It has not resurrected
not re-born.

The same massive rock
hung in my dark sky
reminding me every night
I'm still here
time may veil,
time may unveil,
but the heart,

the heart is still.

STRATEGIES

In adopting new strategies to forget you,
setting new thresholds:

higher levels of bearable sadness
lower levels of expected happiness,

making it through
crueller nights,
colder beds,

heart adjusting to tighter pains
the way our bodies adjust to smaller homes.

Beggar

She loved a man.

She watched him love another woman,
She watched him father her children,
from a far
where she was allowed to stand
far away from him
with her hand on her lingering heart.
as if restraining it,
as if keeping it from falling off the edge
of her breast.

The hungry homeless beggar looking
onto a loving family
through the icy window of their warm home.

He,
   lived a long,
         happy,
             healthy life.

She,
smiled only
when the wind blew,
imagining it had twirled
around him somewhere before
carrying his scent to the heavens.

Doubt

In between
a doubtful sun,
and assertive rain

a cloud

at times dark and angry
other times white and peaceful.

Doubt;
the flimsy line swept this way and that
in this indecisive emotion,
your door always half open,
your candle even by a faintest wind
always fitful.
And I always holding my breath;

I shut all the windows
I trapped you in,
so you would stay

but you were like the heavy,
noisy bluebottle fly,
you were bashing yourself against the glass,
bashing yourself against the glass
wondering why you couldn't reach
the greener grass out side
even thought it seemed so near.

I understand now
and so I leave all passages wide open
for you,
including heart
and with yesterday's news paper,
I gently shoo you towards the open window

Now you are hysterical with fear, confused
you're trying to get a way in uncontrollable madness

  Thwack!
    Whack !

you slam blindly against every surface
that is in your way

I'm not attacking you, I'm helping you
Don't you understand? (I shout)

Once again
man and woman
lost in translation

FUTILE

The fastened button longs to be freed.
His arrogant heart
will not accept the one size fits all
glove.

She held on to him
the only way she knew how
but he keeps slipping through her fingers
the way a small child
                    resists
                        but then unwillingly
                            relieves herself in public,
                                weeps in shame,
tries but cannot explain why it could not be
prevented.

He loves to know she's suffering
so he asks:

  'What's the pain like?'

            'Toe curling'

She answers him with bleeding eyes.

This love
this crippled, futile love,

        fails miserably when attended to,
           thrives vigorously upon neglect.

SOUL'S WINDOW

If our eyes were our soul's windows
the breathing air to the long contained animal
imprisoned by our bodies,
it is then easy to comprehend
why when I see you
I stop and stare.

My soul overwhelmed,
finds its familiar beloved view
puts its life bearings to rest
gazes peacefully,

I feel it
almost rising within me
fighting the urge to step outside
its cage.
reaching its invisible hand
doubtful and longing to leap
and run to you
to sit at your feet
as it used to.
but I think it knows that you
will know it
that you can see it.

Uncertain,
it approached, then retreats
it restrains itself
believing you'll recognize it

after all,
we never forget
those whom we've burnt.

COFFEE

She remembers it
the first time
after the dreams had foundered
maps of life, re-drawn
adequate time passing
to heal
or to enact pride.

Nervous,
she took off her wedding ring
and wore it on her right
finger.
He, referred to his wife
as 'She'.

They sat for coffee
they spoke of politics
and the weather,
but when their thoughts
embraced,
their like mindedness
surfaced,
and their hearts
screamed,
he held his lips
with another sip.
She turned her eyes down to
his fingers,
his thumb and index
tightly wrapped around the
china blue handle
in an intense encounter.

She remembers it
the first time
his passionate fingers
wrapped around her waist,
intense.

Holes

Plucking violently, suddenly
the rusty staple from
the familiar binding it had braced
for so many years,
has left a clear trace.

No matter how many times the pages were
photocopied,
despite outstanding filtering software
the frail yellow papers have surrendered
to the clench of the invasive metal.
Their exposures to its holes has become
a dependency.

The redundant staple
lies there,
worthless and vain.
without the subject of its clutch,
without its enabler,
it could not grasp,
its arms left stretched and open,
in hope.

The evil drug unwillingly
withdrawn from the addict's ill blood,
the malignant cancer cell extracted,
the pitted tooth pulled,
the toxic weed detached.

I can feel your memory receding from me now,
           slowly,
               painfully
                    hesitatingly,
How many years will this one take?

THE WRECKAGE

Why do you come here?
there's nothing for you here
in this old wreckage.
What is it you look for?
What is it you hope to find?
You convince your lingering self
'maybe I've missed it the last couple of hundred times'
dragging the many unhappy years
pictures linked to words, linked to scents, linked to
rain
the rapid, nervous turning of the yellow deteriorating
page,
or do you foolishly believe that something has
changed?

Nothing ever changes here,
only scattered rubble of a few confounded memories:

his smile,
the way the sunlight bounced off his beautiful face

perhaps the heart you lost,
right here,
right then.

The Heart and the Subsidiary

When the heart has grown weaker and frailer with
age,
or when communication becomes more complicated
and difficult,
the heart cowardly hires one of its foreign subsidiaries
to spare it some of the motions, some of the aches:

Tongue: one of the worst interpreters of the heart,
ever.
Lips: a good but confusing agent.
Eyes: a very well equipped attorney, but often ends up
revealing too much.
Brows: vague, and can easily be corrupted by the eye.
Hands: lethal.
Body: not to be trusted, can be very harmful, used
only when absolutely necessary
but still very often.

each with a tool,
each with a skill,
each for a time,
each for a love broken,
damaged,
dumped.

Different languages all uttering the same thing,
I love you, but I can't.

Moth

We are never the same after love.
The fragile moth captured by its delicate wings
(twitching)
our rubbed off velvety scales
forever lost
our detainer's fingertips
forever stained.

We spent what's left of our years fluttering
around the glowing bulb
drawn to artificial warmth.

About the Author

Born in Kuwait October 1980. Fatima did her bachelor degree in Law at Kuwait University.
After graduating she practiced law and journalism until 2005 when she moved to the UK to
pursue her postgraduate education, she is currently doing her PhD in Economic Law at Warwick University. Fatima lives in Coventry with her four year old daughter Jori. Her poetry has appeared in several English Literature Journals and has been shortlisted for the Torbay Poetry Award.

Photo taken by Mohammed Isam Atari.

Lightning Source UK Ltd.
Milton Keynes UK
11 February 2010

149906UK00002B/7/P

9 781449 069360